ELDER

David Constantine was born in 1944 in Salford, Lancashire. He read Modern Languages at Wadham College, Oxford, and lectured in German at Durham from 1969 to 1981 and at Oxford from 1981 to 2000. He is a freelance writer and translator, a Fellow of the Queen's College, Oxford, and was co-editor of *Modern Poetry in Translation* from 2004 to 2013. He lives in Oxford and Scilly.

He has published ten books of poetry, five translations and a novel with Bloodaxe. His poetry titles include *Something for the Ghosts* (2002), which was shortlisted for the Whitbread Poetry Award; *Collected Poems* (2004), a Poetry Book Society Recommendation; *Nine Fathom Deep* (2009); and *Elder* (2014). His Bloodaxe translations include editions of Henri Michaux and Philippe Jaccottet; *Selected Poems* by Friedrich Hölderlin, winner of the European Poetry Translation Prize; *Hölderlin's Sophocles*; and Hans Magnus Enzensberger's *Lighter Than Air*, winner of the Corneliu M. Popescu Prize for European Poetry Translation. His other books include *A Living Language: Newcastle/ Bloodaxe Poetry Lectures* (2004), a translation of Goethe's *Faust* in Penguin Classics (2005, 2009), and a monograph, *Poetry* (2013), in Oxford University Press's series *The Literary Agenda*.

He has also published four books of short stories, and won the Frank O'Connor International Short Story Award in 2013 for his collection *Tea at the Midland* (Comma Press), and is the first English writer to win this prestigious international fiction award.

DAVID CONSTANTINE

ELDER

BLOODAXE BOOKS

ISBN: 978 1 78037 098 9

First published 2014 by
Bloodaxe Books Ltd,
Highgreen,
Tarset,
Northumberland NE48 1RP

www.bloodaxebooks.com
For further information about Bloodaxe titles
please visit our website or write to
the above address for a catalogue.

Supported by
ARTS COUNCIL
ENGLAND

Cover design: Neil Astley & Pamela Robertson-Pearce.

Printed in Great Britain by Bell & Bain Limited, Glasgow, Scotland, on
acid-free paper sourced from mills with FSC chain of custody certification.

ACKNOWLEDGEMENTS

Acknowledgements are due to the editors of the following publications in which some of these poems first appeared: *Agenda, The Best of British Poetry* (2012 and 2013), *Between Almanach (Gdansk, 2013), Oxford Magazine, Poetry London, The Reader, The Rialto, Resurgence* and *Saudade* (an anthology of fado poetry).

CONTENTS

1

How will they view us, the receiving angels...?

How will they view us, the receiving angels
Who perhaps find it easier when the dead are shipped in smoothly
Headfirst, arms across the breastbone, smiling
As if all along this is where they had wanted to be
How will the angels receive our kind
Who will be dragged in feet first, face down, hands
Far outstretched, the broken nails
Black with the dirt of some local habitation?

Old Town

Old town, dirty old town
Thirty-five miles from the sea
But from there to us
Through the buttercup fields and the moss
The big ships crept
And stepped up the great canal
Trailing gulls, and believe you me
That was a sight to see!

Dirty old town
Smog in the mornings, the buses came
Like timid beasts being led
By Master, the bus conductor,
Walking slowly ahead.
And when we came home
Wide-eyed from the glittering Christmas pantomime
Oh the lamps had haloes of rain.

The big ships passed
Big as tenements through
The placid cows in the fields
And there was a lock
We could bike it to
Where the jovial idle singing sailors threw
Us oranges down
That were meant for market in the dirty old town.

And courting couples rode home
On the top of the Number 9 bus
From a Sunday walking out
In the bluebell woods.
Oh armfuls of bluebells came down
Like streams from the slopes of the hills
Into the dirty old town.

A local habitation

Foreknowing the absence – that one day elsewhere,
Not here, oh very far from here, you will look up
And, missing something, for one split second not
Know what it is and through that heartbeat's gap
The sea will pour in that was always near

The tide of everything will break on you,
All manner of love and its own bodyweight
Of grief – foreknowing that, promise me this:
When the agent holds his hand out for the keys
And calculates the worth of emptiness

You won't unwish one thing we did but wear
Them all like beautiful impurities
In the soul's crystal and never wish we'd sat
With the wise on their dead benches on the quay
And watched our ship of fools put out to sea.

*　　*　　*

A man I knew, a young man back then
His childhood got him used to moving on
So he lived warily and when a good thing stopped
You'd see him close his face on it and pack
What he'd be needing next and not look back.

I will look back. I don't forget. Here I am still
Laying up the unforgettable on earth.
I learn and learn, I cannot get my fill
Of you and here and you in the here and now.
When the angels bend my dirty fingers back

They'll see the earth ingrained under every nail,
Stigmata of your nipples in each palm
And lovely harsh ghosts of your pubic mound
That so fitted. They'll contemplate a face
Glaring with all the beauties of this place.

*　*　*

To make a man not mind being over there
They should have barred him many years ago
From gardening in pleasant plots down here.
I've studied the scores of ways that things that grow
Employ against uprooting. Some thrust down

Their forks an arm's length deep, some trail
And cling on other rooted things, some cleverly snap
Leaving their living in. So many ways
Of saying I like it here. Myself with tar,
Mint, samphire, thyme and what's between her thighs

Scenting my fingers I learn better how
To get the black earth to bring good things forth
We'll like to eat next year. I'm too ingrown
In her and here to move out further than
The tide the moon drags out and lets back in again.

Swallows on the island

This early morning again into our small space of air
Like thoughts from nowhere from across salt water
The swallows arrive, voracious, and like the imagination's
Sudden joyous connectings fall to feeding

And the hunted dots of life like invisible particles
Or galaxies are sprung into proved existence
By the turbulence they engender in the visible
Hunters. All that is there. All that food. To think like that

Razor-quick, let alone body out the hurrying idea
On wings so pointedly how much more hungry than I am
Must I become? The thing in view, they seem by a force of
Their own making to be fended clear of hedges, rocks,

Posts, the rooted tree, the placid horse and in the pack
Of their own kind never hit against another
But each stitches alone in three dimensions, all
In concert making a work your retina cannot hold

Still or the brain fathom. But what you can observe
And try to get the hang of is again and again their splitting
The second on a hesitation before an upwards, down
Or slant new departure, that, the gap in a rhythm,

Space (one of their heartbeats) between a then
And a next, watch closely. They will not stay. A couple of days
Ingesting vigour and we shall see them rocking on the wire
As though it were autumn. They'll be gone away

All those handfuls of heart, nerve, appetite, over more
Unnourishing water to some lucky thatch or sweet
Dust and darkness of a barn and a family of humans
Whose year, emptying of hope, would sadden badly

If they didn't arrive. Our rock here is a landfall.
On the still nervous air the need and the grace of swallows
Continue imaginable for an hour or so. Love?
Nothing in a swallow says, I don't want to leave this place.

Love story

Head of the valley or his head, all one –
He had come there hunted, though the mouths, teeth, smiles,
The tongues, the howls, the ferocities coming on and on
Were, you will tell me, his imagination –

But the tree he lay under, finished, staring, that was real,
A real hazel, and the pool it stood flourishing by, that pool
Was the crown knot of the thirteen unique waterfalls
Making and unmaking, deep, deep, always on the boil –

Not that he grasped it, all he grasped was he had come
To the end now, to a place there was no exit from
Up under thirteen falls which were too sheer to climb,
He was done for, let them tear him limb from limb,

He must sleep – And only when he slept and began to dream,
Only when he had given himself up did he begin to know
He had come where he would have said nobody ever came
Who was only as good or bad as he was – up the one stream

To the pool where angels met and gossiped before going down
Into the everyday world with their messages – Quite soon
Perhaps when he can't tell the dreams he has called his own
From the dreams in a hazel nut he will begin to feel

That the things he could not say or never dared to say
Are being said at last by the waters and by the angels getting away
With their good and bad news for people who live downstream
And he will not rejoice, nor will he grieve, he will stay

Where he is now, feeding the roots of an ever more beautiful hazel tree
By a pool in which waterfalls and angels come and go
And when at long last love's messenger, the hoopoe
Arrives with a message for him, only him, at the rendezvous

The hazel who has seen the angels staring at her wet in the sun
Dripping soft gold, flashing garnets, Bird, she will say,
That message for him from far far away and long long ago
He said we were one flesh, he and I, so just as well tell it me.

Under Samson Hill

But under the hill the bright yellow apples are not shaken
Nor a leaf moves, on every lichened twig
How the apples shine and the soft ground below them
Pale gold likewise. So quiet, the only breath of wind

Under the hill our breathing. But out there a kiteman
Is travelling the shallow water, he leaps, he can fly
He can hold on one-handed, raising the left
To salute himself and the wind, fast and ferocious

The wind and the waves stampeding over the flats
And a clever man rides them standing, he lifts off
Clear from their backs, he sails, he is a visitant
He is the glance and dazzle of an angel. And we are

So still here under the triple tree under Samson Hill
I think I will see you even in December, love
On your open palms in the wintry lichen light
Offering me the small bright yellow apples.

L'amour, la mer

L'amour, la mer, it is an ancient trope.
  She slept at once against his heart, he lies
In his thin length of blood and listens to the sea
  That the full moon and the wind northwesterly
Have raised under their window, bed-high.

This lover unsleeping between her and the sea
  His fears have left him, he lies in wonderment
At her who is deep asleep and breathing
  Just as the heart desires in the given rhythm
Of her beloved body's soft insistence

On its repose. And the sea, so close in the little porth
  The pent sea has no room for exhalation
But gulps its own reflux, slops back, thrashing
  And all the roar of the ocean's
Long lunar haul is offered to his hearing bearably

As in a droplet. Proof him, love, a while yet
  Against the clock that is nearer than the sea,
Weigh him quiet, attending, then sleep him down
  Deep with her before he hears and heeds
The clock's dead reckoning, its quartz pedantic metre.

Mirror, window

Before daybreak the window is a black mirror
In which is visible nothing but myself
Looking in. We face each other. He knows
As well as I do what I have in my head
And around the heart. He is not pitiless
Only he cannot help me. I could him.
By looking away at once I could release him
From being on the outside looking in.
I don't, I stare, he stares. It is obvious
We are not good for one another.
I trust he will fade on the crowing of the cock
As he always has and there'll be a world outside
Land, sea and air and some fellow creatures
And I will become invisible to myself
At a window gratefully looking out.

Facing east, at the window

This morning, middle of June, rising northerly
At six the sun passes over my right shoulder
And illuminates the reproduction of a nude
Sixty years ago at an open shutter bowing
Her face over a bowl of water and feeling
The sun on her right shoulder. Landlocked
Why can't I close my eyes and listen for the sea
And bide quiet whatever the season
For a transit of the sun across the nude?

Facing the wall, north

This morning, late November, rising southerly
At eight the sun passes over my right shoulder
And illuminates the map. Switch off the lamp.
Here is at least the area of an illumination.
The place itself might be one of the named,
Popplestone, Puckie's Carn or Hole of the Horse
Or one of the nameless tumuli or the split rock.
Things are more naked at this time of the year.
I should be able to leave this very room
Watchful, concentrating, careful of my step
And map the illumination on to the island.

Elder

Because it lifts up and lays itself open to heaven level
Under sun or hail and out of its warty tubes
You can extrude the soft white marrow to blow darts down
Or finger your breath for Pan and because, if let
It will grace human habitations of a lowly and broken kind
Shapes up nicely to its full never-domineering height
Against a brick wall still standing, curtains a window hole
And altogether does well in places we have spoiled
Abandoned developments, the backs we don't care who sees
And its smell is of the low sort, like hawthorn and rowan
Rank, damp, very much to my liking and because
Elder that is kith and kin with eldritch, eld and that shaft into Hades near
   Castleton
Gives twice, in summer and in the autumn, flowers and berries
And women who remember and have the mothers' recipe
At home in a stained book pluck up an adolescent courage
And return to certain loci let go to ruin
Old corrugated sheds, old bunkers, frightened trystings
And wade in deep through willow herb and michaelmas daisies
And maiden themselves up again with the million cream florets
And redden their fingers with the black roe
From the brimming, the overturning dishes of elder.

On the bridge

Come thus far, trudging, he stops dead and sees
By the sun behind him things that stood in the rain
Unmoved all night, bare stone, bare trees,
Show aspects of themselves that shine

So bright it hurts. Come thus far in
Alerted, warned, the next he sees is her
Riding fast out into the level truthful sun
Radiant, almost brushing him, so near are

Kerb and traffic. Praise him for this, that he
One second loves her without hope or wish to own
Only for her face of beauty and that she
Leaves when she likes. Then he feels fit to join

The drunks who rain or shine sit on the bridge all day
Yowling at girls on bikes who never look their way.

Bad dream

There was a path, the familiar path, the one
I've very often not yet ventured on
Around a mountainside, cut level, a sheer
Fall right, a sheer wall left, a ledge a pair
Might amble hand in hand on round the contour
And there you were, not you, nearest the wall
And there was I, not I, nearest the fall
And you were your age but the hair was wrong
I looked like me but many years too young
And on a bend where this path swung out of view
I, less and less myself, halted with the almost you,
And on the brink, for fun or she dared him to,
He balanced his arms dead level and stood there
On his left foot and over the empty air
Raised level his right and so he stood
Lean steady spirit level of my blood
Over emptiness. You laughed, the pair of you
And laughing hand in hand passed out of view.
On hands and knees, the ledge very narrow now,
I shouted after us, your name, my own.
Yours fled my lips to claim you, like a swallow.
Mine fell between my cold hands, like a stone.

Limestone

Up here, he told me, water is uncertain
Which sea to go for but it does desire
To fall. Down there's the limestone. Knowing you,
He said, you'll like the dales, the way they enter
Dry in the sun through harebells. See down there
That long spur, the scourings either side of it
Are two descending blindly on their point
Of confluence. Soon after that you'll know
What you perhaps forgot in the dry beginnings
That every crack and runnel is water's doing
And belongs to water, you will smell it, you'll
Be under trees feeling through rock for water,
Paws would be better there than booted feet
And best would be the sinuously resolving
Body that belongs there, water's – yours
And mine, so fixed and bony, never multiple
Enough, will hardly do. But still, he said,
The slippy smears of earth on limestone,
The spoor, as they increase and wetten into
Mud, watching your step, your feet feeling
Their way, you'll seem (knowing you) almost
The thing itself coming into life to run
And babble. For a while. But even when you
Concede it's not a path, it is a bed, the
Mint and cressy stream's, not yours, and you
Must move aside, how sweet to walk along
And have a newly risen water for
Companion, all the delights in it entirely
Visible! See what I am, it murmurs
And that I like it. There he paused. And then:
Waters can't rest, one slants into another
Fast and one belonging feeds the next
Which tastes of it. But those two there that mixed

Under the foliage, when they give up
Their twin particularity, that stream,
Almost a river, taking in them and more,
Quite soon as though its heart's secret desire
Were something other than a mapped directive
Into an eastern or a western sea
It vanishes and all the streams that gave
Themselves go down with it. Limestone's
A swallower. Listen when you get nearer,
Lie in the shivering harebells where it's dry
And listen down. An almost adult river
Falls down a hole in the earth's thin crust and all
Its copious white water, widen your eyes
However wide and stare your pupils out
Down there in the dark that river falls through
You would not see the palest shade of it
Nor of the forests and cascades of stone
And shapes of men and beasts that live down there
After their fashion under a cold mucous
And all so beautiful if things nobody
Ever sees as I see you up here in the sun
Are beautiful, he said and stopped. I hope
Never again I'll see a man's face age
So fast and thoroughly and never look
That deep again into the eyes of thirst.

Shameful

Shameful, he said, here the singing birds
Are all in cages. Yes, she answered him
But remember the blackbird on our chimney pot
Who sang his fill of song in at our open window
As we woke side by side. Yes, he answered her

We were lying side by side and over both of us
In equal measure and far beyond
The kindest possible measure of my deserts
Into our waking, wonderfully inventive
The blackbird sang. We were side by side

Hands touching, and I was quite alone
In a lightless head and while he sang
I lay face down at a crack in a concrete floor
And whispering, Welcome, welcome
Out of whichever slow black eddy entertains

The blessed whose faith is not the equal of
Their blessings, the love-deniers
I summoned up my devil whose name is Legion
My progeny, my skewed and squint misfitting
Unholy inventions, my peculiar abundance. I

She said, lay listening sleepily to the common
Blackbird. And I with feelers into hell
In that drenched dawn, in the opalescence
In that unhurrying and reprieving time
All the while I knew that over my vicinity

From every vantage point in freedom
Echoing singing poured. Shameful. If love
She answered him, woke side by side
And under all that singing in the dewy pause
Did nothing, yes, that would be shameful, yes.

Miranda inland

After too long again last night my mirror
Became his eyes in which I saw myself
Thin, stark, desired and all the lore
He offered it me again, the freshets started

Under my heart and I was still the woman
Even inland who understood the tongue
He dreams in, I could hear and follow
And we resumed the mixing conversation

Tides and currents enjoy. His right hand
Fastened on me like a starfish, the feeling
Was vivid orange under the black wrack
Even so far inland. In the mirror seeing

My white self stared at savagely I wriggled
Free and under the deep sea's bedrock slipped
Fast back to his hilly scrap of terra firma
In the wilds of salt and surfaced drinkable.

Idyll

If he never copulated with the sheep and goats he minded
This was because he preferred trees and among trees olives
The older the better, the older the more holes they have
At different heights and angles and of varying depth, sometimes
As many as a baker's dozen he might serve in a single tree
So that one ancient olive grove was a harem for a lifetime
Hundreds of holes every one of which he knew individually
Having bunged them himself with a variety of substances
Variously conducive such as moss, cress, figs and things like feta
Or a choux bun he lifted from the supermarket or now and then
In season for the larger holes an orange which he prepared
Most carefully, enriching the hole within the hole with honey.
People said of this man that he had no ambition, only sheep
And goats all day for very little money. His mother sighed over him
And feared he would never marry. At times it almost seemed to her
He might be a thinker and indeed in his head he was always busy
Remembering and imagining. He was not an educated man
But from somewhere he had heard there were girls and women inside trees
Who had disgraced themselves and he made up names for them
All different and never forgot who was who. Often, crying upwards
He saw how beautifully various is an olive tree's head of hair,
The grey-green watery sunlit tissue of it, the play, the dancing
And the percolation down of the azure, the hyacinthine blue.
He believed his tears were manna. I'd say he was given
The riches daybreak and waking denied the dreaming Caliban.

2

Hydrofoil, fish, gulls

Like a tractor labouring so we, ploughing fast
Drew a tail of gulls. Soon as we rose
In hundreds we flung up fish or, some might say
Fish began dancing, began cavorting and showing off
All the tricks they could do in the breathless air before the gulls
Took them. Purpose
Of our swift skimming, purpose
Of the beak, and between the two, watched from the stern
That spectacle of the fin- and gill-creatures
Mimicking the freedom of *saltimbanques*
In our deadly element
Very beautifully.

The Gate of the Charites

And there they are still just about discernible –
A trace of dance. Oh this town!
That coming into for a lodging or returning home
Or leaving sea-side for your work or to make a voyage
You bowed under their dance. The thought
That either zone, within, without, was theirs
Surely this beautified your bearing.

House by the ancient agora

So you can step down from your garden
And go under the capacious planes and poplars
Into a habitat of terrapins and dragonflies
And many reminders of streets and occupations.
There for example is a place where the nymphs were worshipped
And that is a conduit for the mountain's cold water.
I should think there is more of the old town in your cellar.
You are a later deposit
Still lying awake and listening to the sea.

Pan

In a dip between the north and south hills of the acropolis
Embossed on a rock like a trilobite
And if you clamber up and can hold on the ledge beside him
You will find he is still readable with the fingers
His horns, syrinx, shanks
And there he always was
In a covert between the busy hills of the high town
So close any night or day you might have called on him.

Kouros carrying a ram

He was almost finished when they found a flaw in him
In the stone of him, through the head by his left ear
And broke him in three to be used for walling. Now
In wonder we lift up our eyes to him
Who has been carted down here from the lost acropolis
Cemented back together and stood up before us and who are we
To mind the flaw through his head? That ram
Stepping forward he cups so gently on his right hand
The left arm pressing it against his heart, now pieced together
This long-legged youth for ever stepping forward
Carries that quiet ram to please some higher order
Tenderly to the knife and the flames.

Stele

Erected again among other finds in the sun
It seems not to belong here, like a block the glaciers dumped
And that thing in his grasp that looks like Heracles' club
In truth it is a torch upended
And signifies some ordinary man is dead.
White marble, whiteness of heat and light
How feeble a torch looks at the best of times in the sun.
Under some lettering that recorded who he was
This naked man who lolls here with nothing to lean against
He has dipped the torch, given up.

Marble quarry

Salt crizzles like ice the less and less of water
Till all that's left of the pools that pock the shore
Is salt, crystals of sea, under the sun
That hurts the eyes the way it does off snow.

Into the crucible down the scree lies slant
One temple column they hacked and smoothed for months
Under the furnace sun until they hit the flaw
And they were sent to spill their white sweat somewhere else.

Horse, man and woman, Hermes

Forelegs, head and shoulders entering left he stands
So close behind she feels his breathing on her neck.
He knows this meal will be their last, he sees behind
The facing man she loves and who loves her the cold
Invisible fetcher-in for Death and does the best
He can: stands very close and warms her with his breath.

Sanctuary of the Dioscuri

Knowing the story that during a storm on the *Argo*
Two stars alighted, one on the head of each twin
Sailors since then, at least till the death of Pan
Saw them wreathing the masts with lights when the sky blackened.

A platform barely above the sea; little still standing;
A trickle of shards to the beach. All who sail
Still wish they could have the protection of haloes
And whisper a kind of thanks, all who land alive.

Stoa

Stumps are what's left of the upward reaching but of
The horizontal all's still there to walk out on
And be yourself, the biped, the only upright
Thinking. Ships passing by on other business
Looked to the whole bright edifice for a landmark.
The white sun had an answering shade. But still
On this airy platform, roofless, breathing easy
Might you not step by step so clarify your thoughts
You would not mind them being visible?

Sanctuary

Down here in the mountain's lap, invisible till
Arrival, is where you wanted to come to but
Never could locate. Nor do you know, arriving,
What you wanted here but only that you do still
Want and more. Here is a labyrinth but not one
For solving, it is here to maze you till your blood
Meandering on a watershed decides and pulls
You down. Your heart will stop. It is listening for
The beat Earth keeps herself. The marriage you desire.

Stoa and sanctuary

Both, I want both. I want this terrace in the sun
And a sight of dolphins wreathing the ships that pass
And a thinking clear enough for the distinctions
There visible in the real phenomena
Aptly fine. But also, when you look me in the eyes
As no one does who is not one with me in love
That you see down through clarity into the dark
Sleep maze, where the pulsing leads, the crawl, the cave,
The garnet glow of seeds on the girl's white palm.

3

Orphic

Some of the trees, birds, beasts at his strange audiences
Had once been women and men and when they gathered close
And all through every vein into the heart were listening
Vast, amorphous, puissant as the sea, the grief, the fear,
The various hungers they had lent their bodies to
Shaped up again in them who had no date for this in any
Remembered proper name but certainly it filled them like
A staining, they had pangs and drifts of it, they felt a wraithing
Of what it had been like. Among them other beings
In the present shape of human children, women, men
Felt they could root for moisture, sift the breeze for pollen,
The dreamed command of flying seemed within reach again
Likewise the underwater nosings. Were we the pair
His singing moved to lay their palms down side by side
On a warm and lichened listening stone who saw
The worn gold of betrothal shining under the sun
And felt their own peculiar brevity, their gathered
Accidents in touch and context with a longer life?

Baucis and Philemon

With luck you'll ask, with luck your angel in the giving vein will give
The thing that honours you and the angel best and leaves the world
Your gifts on view, a joy lasting a while. Consider the example
Baucis and Philemon set. Imagine the angel's glee, oh her
Deep satisfaction being asked for that – the aptest gift – and it
Being hers to give. They were weathered by then, they showed the years
They'd lived outfacing, riding, cannily tacking with the whims,
Unfairnessess, pretty cajolings, sudden careless bounty
Of the local weather, they showed its bent, they wore it in their blotches,
Gnarls, scars, dents, they were steeped by that time in the vertical sun
And downpour, sleet at an angle, zephyrs, tempests and they knew
Better than their own the other's texture, juices, smells, blind spots,
Frailties and stocks of patience. All they asked was more
Of what they knew they could. Given the gift, when he saw her
Leaf and she saw him, astonished, leafing, their last words
Were little exclamations, oh and phew and wow, the quick
Intake of breath, the hiss, the gasp and whistlings of wonderment,
Their angel joining in. Not many are so lucky. While they hardened
In bark and branched and finely ramified and crowned, their roots
Felt for the other's roots like toes in bed. So ending, they continued
As trees, outlived their tale, increasing, the angel passing through
The grove thought well of it, thought, There for once I got it right
And some while longer, longer than the angel, even beyond
The memory of angels, they lasted. For all we know beneath
The concrete there's a seed of them one day the fires will wake.

Phaethon's sisters

Grief will do it. The thought of nowhere is unbearable. So grief
Sets off through a world still snowing ash, still smouldering
Through the wide wide world that will be a long time black. Grief
Empties the head of all but the gap and when they came to the still
Unhealthily warm Eridanus and there was a sepulchre
That had his name on it and the one thought had a home
Grief saw no point in going anywhere else. A third of a year
In a world only very slowly cooling they keened over the cause
Him, theirs, the grief, it rooted them, they stayed and kept
His fistful of ash sweet leafing whispering company
For a couple of generations. Some say. Others however
Read the tale differently. In their view Earth, even then
Already sick to death of the Phaethon kind and having had enough
Of his sisters day and night month after month bewailing him
Who did not even (as Icarus did) feed a fish or two but crisped
At once bright pink in the dead-fish boiling river, Earth, they say,
Not vengefully but in her own deep wish against a world of ash
Exacted trees for Phaethon the useless shrimp in his sterile tomb
Three large black poplars offering shade dispensing
A scented coolness and whose thousands of tremulous leaves
Given the least encouragement of the slightest breeze
In drought keep alive the memory of the blessings of rain.
Beautiful trees the sisterly women made and useful.

Daphne

Daughter of a river, she disliked the idea of marriage. Us too,
Her father said, they coop up in cisterns out of sight of the sun,
We turn their wheels, they make us part of their machinery, with us
They slop off the blood, they wash their hands. Is marriage worse? But if
You must, run while you can. So she ran wild through forests, tying back
Her hair with a red ribbon. And it was this, the hair, the slight
Restraint, that piqued the tidy-minded Phoebus. Hair like yours,
He said, should be braided tight, looped up and fixed with pretty
Little silver chains. She heard and ran, pressing her dress into
The parting air and in her slipstream closer and closer, his
Unblinking eyes on the loose red knot, Apollo came, the lover
Of order, ordering her to stop. She ran for home, she ran till she
Could hear and smell and see her river and as the hunter's
Fastidious fingers slipped her silk and his fast breath haloed
Her hair with cold, Father, she prayed, change me, be quick,
Into something he can't have. Peneus did. There on the bank
The hand of Phoebus, grasping for her heart, was kept from the pulse
Of it by bark. For this, he swore, your plaited leaves will garland
The heads of triumphs on the Capitol when I lead them in
Singing. Peneus called his daughter's ribbon, it trickled
Into him. Teach me their language, love, teach me the tongues
And dialects of water and the evergreen breezy leaves,
Lie close, love, whisper me the triumphs and the prizes
Not in the grasp or gift of the god without eyelids.

Myrrha

Any fathers with their nubile daughters here, said Orpheus
Should leave now or if they stay should not believe the story
Or if they believe it should take most to heart the ending, fathers
And their marriageable daughters should dwell on that, the punishment
Not on the crime and all of you, childed or childless, be glad
It happened far away in the east, east of Arabia Felix
And that in our neck of the woods it could not happen. The humans
Did not know how to take this tuning-up but a snigger
Went through the trees, the beasts, the birds. A god swallows his spawn,
A woman proffers her wet bottom to a bull, they had heard it all
And some for things in that line had themselves been translated
So why make such an example of their sister Myrrha, you,
By one woman twice bereaved and now only loving boys
Tell us, singer of Cyparissus, Ganymede, Hyacinthus
What is so special about our little sister Myrrha?
The humans were very uneasy in this knowing company.

Consider the family, he began. Her father Cinyras was
The son of Paphos whom Pygmalion fathered on Galatea
His stone idea born of revulsion at the vile Propoetides
Who snubbed Aphrodite and laid themselves out publicly
For money and she, the goddess, turning them to flint and seeing
Her loyal sculptor night after night wasting his seed upon
The lovely cold unopening mound of Galatea
In pity turned her from stone to flesh as warm as the Propoetides
Had been but wifely, motherly, faithful. See where it ends
When the Goddess of Love takes an interest in you.

The day that Cinyras told her he would soon dispose of her
In the usual way in marriage, that day Myrrha, much as a poet
Or a sculptor, after years travailing at it hard inside
Shoved out into the sun the thing now undeniable.
There it stood. When he took her in his arms and petted her
And said, You must, she saw it the way a mother does when from

Between her legs is reached and given her to hold a creature in its
Blood and clay she knows is hers. The fact, apparent, engendered by
Their eyes and not to be undone. She saw it, he would not. So when
He asked what sort of man she'd have for her fatherer of a child
She answered, One like you. Cinyras was flattered.

                                                      Women have smothered
Or launched in a little boat towards where it might be found
The life they felt they should never have conceived but Myrrha
For three nights nursed it against her heart and called up in its favour
Examples from the animal kingdom of love and copulation
Between sisters and brothers, mothers and sons, daughters and fathers
And among humankind were there not societies, far away
In the west, it is true, or the east, but travelled to and attested
Where that was done? Two sisters, she recalled, their mother
Having been turned to salt by a god, they drowsed their aging father
With wine and first the elder then, next night, the younger milked him
Of his seed and carried it off smiling in their belly-pots. Well done,
Said the god who had left their mother to be licked by animals.
Myrrha cursed the accident of her birth in a narrow-minded place
But in the third night lost the argument with herself
And would have removed the thing from view by closing her eyes
Had not the nurse who slept on the threshold heard her gurgling
And cut her down.

                    Strange and terrible is the love of ancient nurses
For other women's babies handed them to suckle, it is a love
Brought up from under into the big house, they surface full of milk
Into a world of conventions and decorum, they are already
And always old and, like Myrrha's, most are nameless. Stories
Come down through them, the matrilinear line of hired mothers,
And Myrrha's nurse blindly for the truth of it without forethought
Continued hers, that the noose had interrupted. Uncovering, she said
By this white hair, by these emptied breasts, by their milk spent on you,
By the cradle I slept alongside and woke to your least snuffling,
I implore you, say why.

But this, the second time, was harder.
What she had said to herself so that it stood there naked for her
And him too, surely, to see, she had rammed back in again
Throttling the exit with a cord and only as if with forceps
Suggestion by suggestion – a spell? a malady? wanting a man
Her father would not let her have? – could the faithful nurse
Drag it out of her. Then they looked at it and looked at one another
And seeing her child resolved to die the nurse as loyal as tides
Are to the moon and millions of wriggling ocean-swimming elvers
Are to the one high inland pool she promised by Hecate
And by Persephone Myrrha should have the one the letters
Of whose noun her tongue, teeth, larynx and necessary spittle
Refused to assemble. And through her soles she felt a tickling:
The Under-Earth's goodwill. The rest was practicalities.

Came the autumn festival of Demeter. Cenchreis, wife of Cinyras,
Mother of Myrrha, absented herself with other wives and mothers
For nine nights, all women together, fasting from their husbands
To celebrate the mysteries, wreathed with corn and dressed in snowy white.
Cinyras alone and drowsy with wine had a visitor,
Myrrha's nurse, who said: There is a girl in love with you.
She desires you to have her. Will you? – How old is she? Cinyras asked.
As old as Myrrha. – And as beautiful? – Yes. – Then yes, said Cinyras.
Sleep, said the nurse. Sleep and dream in profound darkness.
After an hour or so I will bring her to wake you.
To Myrrha she said, Be glad, I have got you what you wanted.
And she put her hand on the girl's heart and said, There – feel.
It is what you want and I have got it for you. Myrrha stared,
She let the nurse bathe and perfume her and dress her again lightly
And she stared, her eyes widened, she looked to be sucking in
All the coal-black in the universe and thump, thump, thump
Went her heart like drums in the mysteries. Her nurse led her,
They heard the screech owl three times and three times the girl stumbled
But she had in her now the resolve of black water when it knows
The weir is coming, it settles, makes no unnecessary sound
But gathers itself into a smooth deep speed, all of it now

Wants nothing but to hurry over. Some say the moon hid her face,
The stars retracted their small lights, Erigone whom the gods
Set in the heavens because she hanged herself from a tree
In unbearable grief over her murdered father's grave,
Blushed black and vanished. But I say imagine rather
The fast river of desire in Myrrha, the darkness of that,
The will to go headlong over the black slant weir, her bloodbeat
Monosyllabic: yes, yes, yes. Cinyras felt two hands:
One cold, almost skeletal, the other soft, long-fingered, oiled
And gripped tight. It was his daughter being handed over.

The borders are permeable, there is some seepage, some bleeding
Between the kinds, some mutual staining. To the stone, the poplar,
The hyacinth, spider, bear who had once been human
This was a trivial commonplace. Compared with their crossings
What was a running of the colours of love? So they watched the fathers,
Daughters, mothers and sons with amusement and saw them
Staring straight ahead as though by fastening on the singer
(Himself so melting) they could hold the lines. He sang of Myrrha
And told them she knew full well what she was doing but left them
Wondering about her father. Was it his custom and a thing
Man and wife understood, that he would get through the nine nights
Of her absence in the mysteries of Demeter with a bedmate
And naturally a younger? And if he called her 'child'
Was this any more than a ready endearment? Cinyras
Breaking gently (he was practised) into Myrrha's youthfulness
Felt youthful himself. He had obeyed the wine and the nurse,
Slept deep and dreamed and down there in that zone time
Has never been told it must move on.

                                    In the big trangressions
One coupling is usually enough. God's rapes, for example,
Are as fast as sparrow-hawk kills and away he glides, pads, slithers
And leaves the elected female carrying. But Myrrha crossing
Knew it would not be said in her favour she only stayed ten minutes
On the other side. The threshold was alarmed, she had triggered

The Furies, they would come for her in their own good time.
They are never merciful, said the nurse, but they are very busy.

And so next morning before it was light enough for him to see
Who the woman as young and beautiful as Myrrha was
She left him and as his semen laced with a small libation of
Her blood ran cold down her warm thighs she bent the deities
Of Hades and the sky and all the local spirits the way
Of her determination: him, again and again, until
They must call time. To her nurse she said, I see how good this is,
How good a woman and man could get at this. I will learn fast
So he will starve without me afterwards and – who knows? –
Come looking for me wherever I am sent. I begin to feel
How enjoyable I am and how I might be more so. Therefore
Pray to the mothers and the sisters you come from who are below
To encircle me against scruple, conscience, failure of the will
To make my womb the hot aquarium for his shoals. The nurse
Promised faithfully. Myrrha slept, idled and dreamed away
Her hours of daylight, she was besotted with night, oh deep
In love with it, its clever hands, its lips, its numerous ways
Of fitting her. So it went on, night after night, on some
Exponential curve of want, have, be, until the ninth. That night,
The last, for the first time Myrrha allowed herself the sleep
That lovers who have tired one another innocently
Take as their due blessing or perhaps she believed
Closing her eyes she would become invisible or she prayed
That daybreak would be late as Zeus commanded it to be
When he slept with chaste Alcmene in the form of her husband
But it came as usual and there between the flung-wide curtains
Arrayed in the shrieking sunlight stood her father naked
His face like a pit of snakes of loathing and malediction.

Myrrha saw her death coming and suddenly did not want it
So perhaps – the story is full of holes – he hacked the nurse
To bits instead. No one believed his tale of a vile deception
Least of all his wife returning from the mysteries of Demeter

And the autumn sowing. He never could look her in the eyes
After her absences, he felt a smallness, she was abstracted,
She wore the look of having sojourned in the figurative
And what he had done at home among the incidentals
Had never much concerned her till now. He might have said
This time wherever you were, in some such otherish place
I was too and I think I shall be there for ever more without
My mixed companion, my new spouse, and without you either,
The lawful, who will not miss me. When Myrrha left
It opened up a fissure between Cenchreis and Cinyras
Through which vapours writhed as they do in the Campi Phlegraei.
The house in all its rooms and the garden stank of love and blood.

Demeter wandered the wide earth after her daughter
Enquiring everywhere for clues and taking no interest
In anything but the loss. She had so keen a purpose,
So touching, Earth pined away with her. But Myrrha fleeing
Did not know why she had not stood still to be cleft
By her naked father when daylight broke into the bedroom
And armed him with lightning against his own flesh and blood.
She had no enquiries to make of anyone, no whereabouts
To ask for but trailed in mortal danger, begging food now and then
In such a puzzlement that at the door or the window
She must have seemed a creature it was your duty to succour
A peregrina it would be a horror to harbour
But you must not harm, you must not assist her to die
And passed along like this, fugitive, tabu, incognita,
After some days and nights she came to the western seaboard
Of her father's paradisal island, and for one silver coin
Bearing his head, she boarded a slim boat with eyes on the prow
And it was then in transit, crossing into Arabia Felix
Under two supervisions of the sun and one of the cold moon
It was during that passage in silence out of Panchaia
That the thrill of a reason started again in her
As she got away from Panchaia with her swag of seed.

– So I am abhorrent to him, I am an abomination
And not fit to see the sun, nor will I beyond the time
It takes for the nine nights of his seed inside the cave of me
To ferment into a child and while it is doing that I will trek
As an utter foreigner in Arabia Felix
Until I come to the place where the babe will come into being
And I will stop. But meanwhile to answer him back
My father and lover who wanted to immolate me
On the altar of his untruth I will dwell in my mind
And in all the places of this young body he so enjoyed
On that, the enjoyment, on how kind and instructive
Black night was to us, how we learned, how we were getting to know
Things most never have the wit even to wonder about.
I will love him and be glad I have got away full of him
The liar. – So, more or less, she did, heavier and heavier
Trailing the wonder of her like a comet's tail
Through oases and small dirt villages in Arabia Felix
With their groves of venerated and useful trees.
She was given food and water and ushered along in horror
And pity so that no particular place with a name
Should have the onus of her. At the due time then
When the heaviness weighed too much she halted and prayed
A prayer so tactical the deities smiled and nodded
And answered it fast. Not wishing, she said, to offend
The living a moment longer than I must, not wishing either
To go below and be shunned by the squeamish dead, let me die
And live here as something a mother would let her daughter
Linger near and the ghost of a crone come up visiting
In hag moonlight would not curse. – Thereupon, feet first
From under the toenails she began to be fastened
Into the black earth, she felt herself finely deepening
Into nether levels of sustenance till she had a hold
On a life that would outlive her father's house. Then her hair
That he had breathed in the scent of, gasped his breaths into,
Deepened the darkness over his eyes with, and her fingers, her long
Cool fingers that he had interlocked with his, on whose palms

He had practised the art of beckoning, whose aptitudes
He had discovered to her and to himself, all that of her
Flourished outwards and upwards and began to breathe in its own way.
Shoulders, breasts, belly, the tousled mound, the intricate
Entrance, all that he had begun to learn and to teach
Was sealing up, hardening over, she was passing beyond
His poor grasp, he would have had to begin again with her
And everywhere his understanding would have failed.

Still it was not finished. Even as she fixed and stiffened
She felt the reason in her insisting she must bend
And keep a while longer the possibility of opening
So that the heaviness which had slowed and stopped her walking
Should not lie in her for ever as a deadweight
And before her features were lost in the markings of bark
Before her mouth clotted she began the crying of a woman
On Eileithyia whose friendship to women is unconditional
Who sides with them and the child, always and everywhere
Does her best for them. This goddess kneeled before the tree still trying
As a woman to kneel, held open the closing carapace,
Reached out the boy on a scream and laid him below her on the earth:
The boy Adonis who would grow to be an astonishment
And be shared in love by Persephone and Aphrodite
And be run through by a boar tusk and gush from the groin
And seed himself abundantly down Earth's slopes and in her hollows
As red anemones. His mother grew and her kind still grows
In Arabia Felix on hard ground, much sun, small rain, feeling
Through stones for the necessary damp. She weeps a resin
Whose threaded tears young women wear as necklaces.
They scent the dark. They lessen pain. They increase desire.

Erysichthon and his daughter Mestra

What better narrator than a river? Those travellers
Thwarted by floods from proceeding and invited in
By the river himself out of the shapeless land under water
Some days and nights they holed up snugly in his cave
And feasting, sleeping, dreaming they listened to wonders
In through the labyrinth of the ear, into the heart's own riverways
The fabulist Achelous poured them stories
So that thereafter and always wherever they were
If they listened they heard the whispering of waters, lifelong
An undulant fever ran in them whose thirst was for stories.

Yes, said the rivergod, raising himself up on an elbow,
King Erysichthon lived in a good place, fruitful
Among waters that were so to speak the twigs and branches
Of my dear brother Peneus but unhappily
He had a passion for banquets and desiring
A hall as capacious and intricate as his appetites
He trespassed for timber into Demeter's grove
With men, ropes and axes. An oak grew there, nine dryads
Close and reaching round to join hands measured the girth of it
Demeter's dearest, hub, crown and glory of that sacred wood
Dressed with half a millennium of prayers and thanks
And this tree Erysichthon chose for the joists and jambs,
Lintels and rafters of his eating house. Birdsong ceased
And a woman's voice – all heard it, many said afterwards
It was the voice of the goddess herself – warned him politely
Don't. But he spat on his hands and answered back: Were this
Not just a tree she delights in when she saunters here but her very
House and home, still it falls to me, I will have it. She gave him
One last chance: as he raised the axe that vast tree from top to toe
And out to the leafing finger limits of every branch and twig
And in every nestled acorn blanched, shuddered, the green underwent
A whitening like a stroke of frost and a voice – all heard it

And all said afterwards it was the small frightened soul
Of the gigantic tree, the butterfly delicate anima –
Begged him, Don't. But he swung and with all his strength
Brought the blade down slant into the bark. Blood gushed as though
He had axed a black bull for a sacrifice and his men
Grey-white and quaking like the tree went on their knees entreating
Sir, don't. Erysichthon prodded one with the heft:
You, do it. And lopped, when he refused, his shaking head,
Showed it to the others by the hair and staked it on the sidelines
Watching, to encourage them. They took eight hours and when
Demeter's oak was notched three quarters through and the blood
Had dried around it in a wide black skirt they roped it high
In the necks and over many arms and backing off far
They heaved till it keeled and at first slowly then like an avalanche
With speed proportionate to weight fell destroying
A large stretch of the sweetly sylvan. All heard, all saw
All were agreed at this demise the wide-eyed spectating head
Screamed and rose from its perch through the colossal debris as a crow.

There was a pause during which King Erysichthon
Munching the summer's figs and peaches from a satchel
Contentedly watched his men making beams of Demeter's oak.
The hewers themselves slept badly, they sidled to their wives
With fearful questions: blood in your milk, any whiteness
In your monthly blood? They heard voices: polite Demeter's,
The tree's terrified soul. They heard the head of their workmate scream.
In the time allowed they raised up the shape of a hall
Large enough to accommodate any known human hunger
The bare white skeletal frame of a royal megaron
And there it halted. For in that interlude the evicted dryads
Had cloaked and hooded themselves in crow-black gossamers
And gone in a silent troop to the mother of all, Demeter
And lain before her in a wide half-circle, saying nothing
But so that she saw their grievance and the earth under mourning
And bringing home the insult done to her. She nodded,
They trailed away through exile after a hope of trees

53

And Earth herself, then on the crest of her bounty
Abundant enough to feed every living needy creature
Tremored at the knowledge of what was coming to the King.

Demeter sent for a messenger, an oread, and said
Since, as you know, I am prohibited by the Law of Life
From being in the same place as Hunger, go, please, on my behalf
Give her my greetings and ask will she be so kind
As to serve my vengeance and visit King Erysichthon
And cram him with her good self. Where Hunger lives, in Scythia
Among the creatures we call the Emaciations
Nobody goes who can help it but nobody
Bidden by Demeter can help it. The oread found Hunger
In a tundra field, scratching. Her skin is as thin as tissue paper,
Trapped under it are bubbles of black blood, she has the belly
And other swellings of drought, her eyes are pools of flies and hang
Below like her exhausted dugs. She spindles along
Like a toddler, old as sorrow, her energy is that
Of bacilli thriving in a phthisic lung. Demeter's messenger
Though she kept her distance and shouted the bidding across
Felt herself to be inhaling invisible pangs.
She wrapped her cloak over her mouth and nose against these spores
And left as soon as Hunger signalled obedience.

Light as dust Hunger came on the winds to Erysichthon
And found him asleep in the house he informed the world
Was the hovel of a man who ate meat once in a lifetime
Compared with the palace he was building of Demeter's oak.
Bare Hunger uncovered and bestrode him, she pinched shut his nose,
Worked open his fleshy lips with hers as thin as nail parings
And blew. He was done for. A while longer she lay
Idly flickering her tongue deep down his throat. Then left him
Dreaming of eating and rode a wind back to her land of famine
And for the rest of the night he practised for the rest of his life
Opening, chewing, swallowing, opening for more.
The food was phantom. He woke, still ignorant, starving. I dreamed

Such a dream, he shouted, such goodies, and I am famished!
Bring me now in superabundance the real thing.
They did. He fed. It made him ravenous. She of the tundra
Where there is no warmth in the sun had given him fire
And fire the more you feed it the more it desires
And roars for more and more. So Erysichthon, a king
All must obey, commanded and got by the cartload
The nourishment his appetite needed for her tyranny.

Make a bonfire of your stock, feed it day and night
Even a king soon wants for fuel. Fire moreover
Hot enough will eat most things but a human's hunger
However keen, however undiscriminating
Hunts in a world that is largely inedible. His ambience
Grazed bare, the seed corn already passing through his gut
King Erysichthon traded the heirlooms. The crows
Observed in amusement the long caravans departing
Piled high with bronze, silver, gold, the precious stones and vases
And likenesses of beasts and people in beautiful white marble
And gleefully flocked over the imports, the heaped
And herded comestibles. The tribe of crows prospered
And Erysichthon at a sitting ate what they let through.
His household fled, they had seen him considering them
As meat. In dreams he became a herbivore, grasslands
Offered themselves and replenished wherever he trod and fed
But in truth the fields were losing heart in his vicinity,
At the turn of the year very little showed above,
The roots he might have boiled refused to signal their whereabouts.
He sat in the house he had called a poor man's hovel
Viewing the white oak skeleton he would never flesh out
And his only company was his daughter, Mestra.

Mestra, said Achelous, and the name lit up his face
As the crossing sun does water, Mestra was in love with Proteus
The Old Man of the Sea, and he with her and why do I say 'was'?
They are, he and she, he gave her with his love the longing for

55

Salt water and she him for the sweet and to help them both
Master of metamorphoses, he shared the gift of it with her
And taught her how. Yes, said Achelous, when she could not bear
The being without him any longer, the full moon nights
She wrapped herself in mist and ran through the water meadows
And slipped in a salmon shape downstream to him or he
When all the sea was one vast loneliness without her
He became a seal and nosed his way upstream as close
As water would allow and lifted her out of sleep by mewing.
Oh that pair knew the rivers and the tributaries
All possible watery ladders! Now, this girl, this nymph the sea
Himself came calling for, her father in the dustbowl of his heart
It crossed his mind as day by day the traded victuals lessened
That he would eat her. He slept on the idea. Woke with a better:
That he would trail her round the wasteland's frontiers
And she, his flesh and blood, would feed him by transactions.

Piety, said the King, her father, demands it. You see my ill
And what you can do about it. You are young and beautiful
Which is to say you are a rich resource. Who knows
You may buy me time enough to discover a fund somewhere
As inexhaustible as my hunger is insatiable
Or the curse may be lifted. Where there's life there's hope
So we shall live in hope. They will soon know us along the borders.
They will pity me and desire you with admiration. Afterwards
The gods may set you in the night sky as they did Erigone
To be an example to other daughters. They began their progress
Mestra and the king with the cavernous bright eyes
Working the frontier, day after day, from house to house
She continued her education in the school of hunger
And in every house they left a feeling of infamy
And longings as keen as the start of a starvation
For Mestra, sold, night after night thought of her lover
Proteus and became to the men who had bought her
Whatever they had hungered for and never tasted
Or never enough. She took a man's head between her hands

And enquired through the eyes into the pit of him
And did not even need to lip-read. Be this, be that:
She interpreted the meaning of every man's wellspring
As at Dodona the priestesses know what the oak leaves are saying
When the god breathes through. Be this, be that, and she became it,
She was for them what they most covertly desired,
She crossed the frontiers, she mixed the decided kingdoms,
She lent the colour of one thing to another, whatever
Crossing they paid her for she delivered it in person,
All the while thinking, My lover would be proud of me,
See how many I am! She marvelled from a distance
Over the tyrannies she released her clients into
Over the multiplicity of possibilities
Eating them. So she fed the thin man her father,
A scarecrow in the rags of royalty, until one night
By a lake, by the lip of the lake where it passes over
Into another shape of itself and makes for the sea
Her father hired her to the thief Autolycus.

Autolycus took her face between his hands. I hear you have the gift,
He said, I hear you can multiply and absent yourself.
Along the road behind you and your father with his one-track mind
(Terrible to have a one-track mind in this world that is so plural)
I have encountered all manner of appetites
Quickened and abandoned so that they do not know what to do.
We are similar beings, you and I, our one big difference
Is that you are beautiful. I thieve and leave people
Bereft of what they owned. You coax into the daylight
What they had never quite acknowledged theirs and I'm afraid
Henceforth they will howl at the moon for it. Into Autolycus
Mestra looked as deep as he into her. She nodded,
Thieve me, she said, I have had enough of servitude
And if you wish to marry me I say yes on this condition:
That you understand I am in love elsewhere and that you
Act towards me accordingly. Yes, yes, said Autolycus
I was already minded to go down to the sea again,

The sea is a great bringer-in of my sort of business
And sometimes I shall be on the run. You will do what you like.
We shall get along very well you and I. And now
Till daylight putting aside your Old Man of the Sea
Show me some of your repertoire. I want to make a song of you
And sing it to the general public on my travels.

People Autolycus robbed rarely saw what they were losing.
He could turn a stallion into a piglet and walk away with it
Bidding the owner good-day. So the next morning
Mestra rode out on his shoulder as a snowy owl.
She's in there sleeping still, he said to Erysichthon.
I must have worn her out. Here is your meal money.

When he saw the empty room Erysichthon knew he was finished.
High summer. He crept home, buying food with the trickster's crook coins
And stripping the fruit trees. Never enough. As he neared the centre
The land blackened, everywhere he saw the curse of his voracity.
Earth was mistrustful. Very little green and succulent
Risked it into the daylight. King Erysichthon curled at last
In the vast oak skeleton of his banqueting hall
Hunger devouring him. He began to feed on the one thing left:
Himself. He was scrawny, he was all gristle, his blood
Was thin and sour. He shrank, tightened, gnawed, his hunger
Worried at him like a pack of wolves but he was a poor meal,
He was less and less, the appetite screamed for more.
The goddess allowed him eyesight almost to the end
So that he saw the timbers leaf around him and over him,
He saw them sprout, branch, run delightedly in all directions.
He lived just long enough to foresee a grove. Yes
Said Achelous, admiring behind the company
Trees waist deep in the shining flood, Autolycus
Sings his song and passes his greasy hat round
And Mestra whistles her lover out of the sea.

4

The Rec

Back home and finding the rec gone
Flogged off, become a gated community
CCTV in every hanging basket
And identical shaven-headed fat men
Aiming remotes each at his own portcullis

How can I make of it a 'luminous emptiness'
As Heaney did of his axed chestnut tree?
It's a space stuffed full with hardware
Loungers and meat. At thirty paces
It lights up sodium white. Pitbulls prowl the wire.

Oh that man who stands at the bus-stop all day long
And whatever number bus comes he never gets on
But tells everybody waiting, It was all fields round here
When I was a boy – day by day, more and more
He's me. I tell them Miss Eliza Smythe left the rec

In trust to the Town in perpetuity
For the health of children, her line dying out.
It was an old enclosure quick-set with hawthorn
And we lay there watching and waiting for our turn
In a team-game on the free ground under the open sky.

Only the moon and stars lit up the rec.
Few still believe there was such a playing-place
But, yes, another elegy would be very nice
So remember all you like. Can we live on lack?
Should have stopped them grabbing it. Should take it back.

Gwyn Robert and the seal

Nature is not only odder than we know but odder then we can know
JOHN BURDON SANDERSON HALDANE

Well, JBS, had your ghost been hovering
That day on the water under Badplace Hill
When the quizzy Old Man of the Sea
Rose to inspect Gwyn Robert of Tan-y-Castell

Who loves worms, frogs, crabbies, you'd have thought
The answering gaze of that boy in the bows,
His silence, wonder and solemnity
Entirely right. Yes, he is one small human

Who'll never suppose the little that shows
Above water is all. Be sure when he finds his tongue
He'll pester the head and shoulders of Proteus
With questions about the rest. And the icebergs

Calving in panic this summer from the warming
Matrix, he'll guess by the stare of their foreheads:
The bulk of their burden, the nine tenths of our
Sad ignorance, is homing on us below.

Our Lady of the Blackthorn and the Snow

She arrived from a place she had found where there was still snow
And set up her stall of love that will never fail
In a place where there'll be no end of the need for dole

She stood in the dirt with her sign, the blackthorn branch
And finger-length were the thorns of her branch
That never flowered in the cold where she came from.

She stood barefoot by her stall and the people queued
In the heat for the dole, more and more they came
With their dead in their arms to the head of the queue

In the dirt, her dole never failed but what she desired
In her heart was the place she had left that was cold, she feared
For her snow. What hope in this world has snow?

The queue came from over the curve of the globe to her.
Surely her thorn will flower in this heat for a day or so
And she will have nowhere to go.

Owls

Wake hearing owls, wake certain
My poor sleep long I have been listening
To the owls calling across me. O my ghostly

Insistent conductors through the shoals of sleep
To the borders here, thus far
No further, go back now

Into the darkness, do not be seen
While I crawl into the workaday fret, while I
Shift badly in the glare of noise

Let me believe you keep yourselves safe in the dark
At the back of my head, my pilots
Sounding across me, calling and answering.

Hölderlin Fragments

I modelled these 'Hölderlin Fragments' on Hölderlin's own
Pindar-Fragmente which he composed in 1803 at the time of
his beautifully strange versions of Sophocles' *Oedipus* and
Antigone. Each of those nine texts consists of a fragment of
Pindar's verse, closely translated into Hölderlin's own late
language, and a passage of prose set below it as though to
explain and comment. But that comforting relationship – text
+ exegesis – is belied by the practice. Out of the fragment of a
poem, elusive in its peculiar beauty, Hölderlin derived a poetic
prose which itself reads like translation from a strange elsewhere
and itself seems to call for exegesis. The whole sense of each
piece is generated in the interplay of ancient text and modern
reading. Resisting exegesis, they reach out from the borders of
his alienation for future readers to continue them.

I translated the verse fragments here from among the many
poems Hölderlin began and could not finish in the four or five
years after the death of Susette Gontard and his being taken
into the clinic and then the tower.

1

Sweet then to live under the high shadows of trees
And hills, sunnily, where the way
Is paved to the church. But for travellers whom
For the love of life, always measuring,
The feet obey, the ways
Blossom more beautifully where the roads...

The trees reach for the sky, the hills even more so; the church itself, fastened hard on the ground, points upwards. And you have settled for the one path from house to house, from yours to His, and can tread it dryshod any afternoon to botanise in His sunny acre and continue your family history among the lichened and leaning stones. Meanwhile every April roads to the four quarters clothe like girls in plum and cherry and quit this hollow and lead out over the hills and far away.

2

                                                                But

Through the garden slinks your fearful
Guest without eyes
Madness. For the way out
Will hardly be discovered now by anyone
With clean hands.

Not that long ago – the Golden Age ? – it seemed the garden
was the best place to be. High wall around, savagery outside.
And here they are in the Age of Lead wondering how to get
out and madness playing blind man's buff among them. State
of siege, the supplies eating up, madness as contagious as the
plague. And as to clean hands, have they forgotten what they
did to make this place? They dunged the ground with blood
and bone.

   Now the wilderness is waiting. It has patience. It has learned
all it needs to learn about the human race. When the cleverest
finds a way out of the poisoned garden and calls to the others,
Tool up, lads, and follow me! the wilderness will be waiting. It
will eat them

3

But when the busy day
Is lit
And on the chain that leads
The lightning down
The heavenly dew of the hour of rising shines
Then feeling climbs
High in humans too
So they build houses
Work starts up
And shipping on the river
And men and women offer their hands
To one another, give and receive, sense
Is earthed and for good reason then
The eyes fix on the ground.

Earth, we assume, can take any amount of lightning. The spires reach up for it and hand it down and in. A phenomenon! Very exciting. But I know people – not many but enough – who seeing the morning dew in everyday radiance don't know what to do with themselves. None of the usual trades will satisfy. I might say beware the hand of a man or a woman reaching for yours with that sort of light in his or her eyes. Then you'll need earthing, the pair of you. Eyes down, the earth can take it. Doubtful if you can any more.

4

But I am hummed about
By bees and where the ploughman
Makes his furrows the birds
Sing on the light. Heaven
Has many helpers. The poet
Sees them. Good
To hold on to others.
For no one can bear life alone.

The beauty of it, that friendly interacting of earth and air and the creatures of earth and air, is also a rightness. Indeed, this fitting together helpfully may be that without which there can be no beauty. The parts fit, they belong and work together, this may be the seed of life in the making of beauty. The beautiful poem is a living example of mutual aid. Even Heaven – this poet says so more than once – needs helpers. So saying, he revolts against the very idea of omnipotence. He extols the cosmos, the dance, the democracy. The part is no good on its own. It makes no sense. It is not viable.

5

Above all spare
The wilderness made
By gods and decreed
Clean to their children to walk in
Among the rocks as they please

Perhaps after all it would have helped to believe the earth
didn't belong to us. The mistake was putting us in charge. So
easy for our kind to pass from that to thinking we owned the
place.

Heatherlands bloom
In purple for you
Lady and dark springs too
For you and your son but for
The others also

The other gods and goddesses and their progeny. At the start
there was a good deal of commingling and nobody bothered
much who your mother and father were, god and goddess or
one or the other with the woman or man next door. All we had
to do was not trash the place.

Or the gods will take back what is theirs
By force, as they would from serfs

Too late now. Masters and slaves. But all the four rivers of
paradise, confluent and directed, will hardly wash the
wilderness clean of us.

6

Terrible therefore over the earth
Diana, huntress, walks and angrily
The Lord lifts over us
His countenance brimming with
No end of signs. The sea meanwhile
Sighs when he comes

Implacable when outraged, sister, don't forget, of Apollo who stood by the ships and loosed the arrows of plague into the packed army of the Greeks, she, Diana, Artemis, huntress, walks the earth and does not like what she sees. And over the rooftops, hills, forests and out of the level sea the flat white face of the Lord himself is rising. Now even the stupidest know what he means. The oceans, three quarters of the surface of the globe and increasing daily, sigh. Still, view things anthropomorphically if you must. Say that the salt water, out of which love stepped, sighs with relief that now it will soon be over. Not even the stupidest will suppose that the waters are sighing in pity for us. But relief or pity or the murmur of awe at the advent of Artemis and the Lord – all nonsense. In truth the sighing is the seas coming to the boil.

7

Meanwhile let me walk
And pick wild berries
To quench my love for you
On your paths, o earth

You might walk to botanise or to see the world or to lay your worn-out boots on the altar of Saint James in Compostela. Surely not in the wish to quench your love. Besides, earth whets the appetite she feeds. Walking her paths and browsing on her berries won't quench your love for her. And why should you wish it would?

Late summer, the paths are open, the berries are plentiful. Enjoy the meantime. Walk, eat while you can, shut-down and dearth are coming. And of course this may not be only the usual winter. Perhaps the wish for quenching is pre-emptive, to suffer less. Perhaps he is thinking, I'll walk while I can and browse on the berries of the earth and pray I can walk and browse so much I'll have had enough and staying at home under the clock tower in the everlasting winter will be bearable. Lessen your love, grieve less.

This bright morning, I'll think the meanwhile is meant to last for quite some time and that the lover's purpose in ambling and striding out in it is to prove and be glad of what he knows already about his love. He is lean and alone, he carries very little, he strides along, he feels on a day like this he could walk for ever. His mouth is stained with berries.

5

Foxes, rain

Waking I heard the foxes in next door's garden.
They have eviscerated a black bag.
They are hungry, they want to live as long as possible.
And I dozed, woke again, heard only the rain
And could not imagine it other than black
Falling hard, a copious black rain. I hope my friend
Is not lying sleepless tonight. He has no appetite,
He has pain, he lies during daylight in the living room
Under a blanket by the fire and can't get warm.
Daylight today will crawl out nearly dead
From under an inexhaustible cold rain.
My neighbour parting his curtains will be sickened
How much there was to eat still in his guts.

Bread, full moon

The warm bread we were handed this morning
Came with the story it was baked by moonlight
The full moon so close, so brilliant
Electric would have looked no better
Than candles in the sun and he worked the flour
And fed the pale loaves into the hot dark
All by moonlight and this cold morning
His wife handed them to us with the story.

By 4.30 when the baker entered his workplace
And saw he could bake the day's loaves by moonlight
And that it would make a story, elsewhere
My friend had lain so many hours and the same moon
So close, cold, brilliant, painful at the window
That all the given names would no longer adhere
To the seas, the lakes, the bays, Nectaris
Went into dust along with Iridium
And beneath the dust where there had been Joy,
Calm, Rain, Fecundity, there was no water
Only vast deserts of cold lava and no air.

He cannot be nourished now by nursery rhymes
Nor by the myth of the goddess paddling ashore
Nor by the story of a woman this bright cold morning
Pressing a loaf of bread that was baked by moonlight
Against her heart, the warmth comes through her clothes,
She breaks off a crust to share with her first child
Toddling along, still a year too young for school.

High tide, early, 19 February 2011

Woke. Did it wake me? Or my hearing
There after all biding quiet and capable
Far down under the din of dreams
Sensed the good moment to listen
For what in the dark is there all along
Far out and biding its time, the moon
The stars, all manner of weather
Any number of hours passing over
And it does not die. Listen
These are the smallest waves
An ocean can make, they are
Not hurled at you, they have whispered in
Up to the lip of the frontier
They share with you and nothing
Is asked of you but that you listen.

The makings of his breathing...

The makings of his breathing are still there
The organs of it are still warm in him
And around us both still is the common air
But the works of breathing have shut down in him

And now we can have no more talk although
The tongue and larynx are still warm in him
And his mouth is open, set as though
Breath and talk might come and go in him

And we'd have conversation as we always did
Taking it up where we left off last time
And speak and listen as we always did
But he has no breath now and we can't resume

For a while after a death...

For a while after a death I live more kindly
To the world and on myself also am kinder. I see
That things I have thought bad, how glad of them
The dead would be, to have the option of weighing
Better and worse, how searchingly they would look
For the good side. Today on the bus when I saw
A young woman see in the looks she got
(This day of leafing and birds building) how wintered
She looked I felt a cold draught from the state the dead
Inhabit who have no chances any more and under
My breath I begged her to be kinder, to believe
The self she was charged with, meagre at present,
Could still flourish. All this ordinary day
I have had the company of my dead friend whose last
Acts and words were all of a kind to leaven
Every gift in us, I have felt him whispering, Watch
For the good and that I look out for him too
Since I have the eyes. So I tend his life and he
Will freight me with it kindly until I fail him.

Cloud opening, 19 February 2012

Cloud opening, the sun that lives in fire
Out there remote as death came over the water
At just the low declension that would work. And all
The makings were aligned in place. A year ago

My friend being on the lip of going over, I
Woke early listening to the whispering in
Of further life. Now this: the day already broken
The occluding cloud was pierced and a cold slant

Of sun cut through the fretted rushes, crossed
The frontier of our salt-drizzled window
And on the wall, close as I am to you, along
The west coast of the island's map, on pale blue

I was shown the ghost of life, life at the quick
In silence hurrying and endlessly in flow
Like the soul of fire, the speeded smouldering
Before flame issues roaring from the heart, almost

Watery, a falls ascending. On our few makings –
Rushes that bind the dunes, glass licked by salt,
Rough skyblue wall – on our few fixities
That last a while, the makers fell, the wind

That scats the rushes ceaselessly, the wind
And cold light from the astral furnace fell and cast
On this room's wall the haste of unending life
So close I could have dipped my hand in it, this hand

The water, fire and everlasting breath of life
That close, the play, the show, one year beyond
His being carried over further off
Than this sweet morning's sun that thrives in flames.

6

Told one of the goldfish wouldn't last the night...

Told one of the goldfish wouldn't last the night
He hid his eyes under a fierce scowl
And went outside on the flags and rode his bike
Round and round, round and round

But it did no good and he brought the fact back in
Heading for his bedroom and his secret stash of chocolate
But his mother got under his scowl and halted him
Till he showed her his eyes and that was that.

So much sorrow there is in a not-quite-five-year-old
They know so much already and suspect the rest
Already they are beyond being consoled
They watch, they have seen it signed and witnessed

That all living creatures have one thing in common:
They die. Creatures as intricate and various
As a worm, a swallow, a cat, a water-scorpion
Baby and grown-up, all of them, all of us

Die. So when in her arms her child became a well
And the waters of sorrow that are under the earth broke through
For a golden fish she was inconsolable
Grieving that his grief was right, just, true.

J.P.

What's gone? A man. Like any. Like none.
He was as local here as Anchor Drang
Or Gweal Neck. The church was full. The cap
He never took off lay on the lid. We sang
For those still in peril on the sea that cannot stop

Muttering. Only ask, tide in, tide out
This swapper of gossip, grapes and crustaceans
A world of ships he would tell you about
The wrecked and the hale, the skippers, the rig
The lowdown and lore of the sea lanes.

And when he was dying and when he was a dead man
The news put out down the sound and into the oceans
And whispering grief came in
On the tides round the field where he lies with his kin
Shut up, a loved man, like any, like none.

As though... because...

As though parting the tamarisks you came down
To the pale lap of sand you love and saw the tide
Backing off from a thing that had swung without a north
For years out there over the cold, a thing

That had lived life as a tree once, rooted, airy, singing
And now the sea delivered it prone into your heart
A caber tasselled with many thousand feeders
Like locks or flaccid legs, some black, some pink as tongues

Or drained to a soiled transparency, each with a glans
Of shell, rimmed yellow, and as though you saw
That this stiff length of life, like a creature born
To run or slither, even if a spring tide came

And clawed it back again, febrile with flies,
And took it out over the curve of the globe away
Will lodge in you for ever, lovely wispy
Though the tamarisks are and firm and clean

The sand underfoot when you strip to swim
You will always know there is a trunk out there
A dead log rolling lost over the cold with life
On it as though it wore its guts and brains

Outside, out-thinking you, and, lying awake,
Hearing the sea, wave upon wave, thought upon thought
Never will you unthink and unconceive it now
As though, as though... because, because, because...

Envoi

The thought that nothing over there at all resembles
Anything over here being unbearable
In disbelief we split you a length of lasting oak
And dig the heartwood out and seal you in its place
With some bright objects you had owned and launch
You face-up, head-first, lidded on the waters
That course under the earth. And having around us still
The gifts of the years of your loving usefulness
We feel a certain hope that you will be elected
To serve among the crew of the Ship of the Sun
Hereafter, as you desired, helping the warm light
That we below surviving cannot live without
Sail on her way. Go now, little boat
Little narrowboat, from the shore of home
We push you out into an ocean wider, deeper
Blacker than anything we have seen or can imagine
And wish for you, thin corpse of our frail kind,
Among your things whose inner light, we trust
Will spring into their life again at the unlidding
Where the Sun Ship lies at anchor, hiring hands
We wish you landfall there at the lightening berth
For the climbing of our sky, we shall imagine you.

A Faiyum death mask

We in our own and local fashion having had
A Cydnus, an arrival, refuse to be shipped off
Faceless under the wraps of death. Love said to me
Slot under the lattice of the bandages a mask
Of her, as true as the arts can make it to the look
She wore when by the river's flood tide she was landed
Here on the shores of the life that you had lived till then
Without her. Show her still and for ever looking up
Alert and curious, taking in your welcome
So that when she berths alone in the unsmiling place
And cannot breathe a word the receivers there will pause
And read her face and marvel at you both precisely.

Tomba 736, una donna, Enotria, VI secolo a. C.

Lady, in the rubble of you, in among
The unstrung vertebrae and bits of rib
And in the vacancy of sex and womb
And either side your skull which looks as frail
As a sea urchin denuded by the sun
Ivory, gold and amber are lasting well
And even iron that rusts, an iron key
Still lies intact where your absent right hand
Had grasped it, woman, female of the human
Species, shape in the dirt, much like a form
Of life that sank into extinction down
To a bed of mud and under centuries
Of drifting silt and under millions
Of pressing rock, so many millions
Of years and more, upheaving and eroding
Till your poor slice of time comes back to light
And a fellow human stares (as though this were
The worst of it) at your missing hand and feels
You left a grief behind that could not bear
To think you'd go where you would not be loved
And dressed you again for sovereignty
In the gifts he had given you, in amber
Ivory, filigree gold, the earrings,
Loops of necklace, low slung belt, and closed your hand
On the key to some fit lodging, lady.

Red on black

I am told this flat land is a vast necropolis
And knowing that, I find it hard to sleep.
The idea works in the earth of me. Like most
Who lie awake I want continuation.

Often at night I think of the Bologna stone.
Lay it for a while in a good strong sun
Shut in the dark then it will shine for hours.
That is its way of breathing in the world:

Give me a deal of sun I will intake it
Husband it in me and give it out again with increase
In places where the very idea of light has gone from mind.
Even more like that are the red-figure vases

Laid up in the tombs for the lucky in life
In the hope their spent warmth would continue
Red on black, their walking together and conversing
Eros and music, episodes from the stories

Shining and tuneful as the constellations.
Often at night my thoughts turn to the looters:
Out of the silent tumuli hereabouts
As from a long-lost kiln they lifted vases

Cold to the touch, the fired beauties,
Delivered them into the continuing sun
The lovers, the singers, the flute players, the dancers
Red on black, cold, cold, outlived by fired clay.

Cast of a woman of Pompeii, Manchester Museum

The woman of Pompeii again, another cast of her
Cast of the mould that was all that remained of her
After the fire and centuries in a stratum where
She dematerialised, exactly vacating her shape
That could be cast. Her only visitor, coming upon her

Here in a hush, it troubled me: she is reproducible
Like any statue, the woman prone, pillowing her head
Coiffured, on her right arm; the sleeve, left elbow, torn;
Tatters of the dress between her shoulder blades; below
All stripped; the woman whose form, the living lines

Of her, from heel to head the soft ash copied close
And shrouded hard. In the present tense of memory
She troubles me. Turn over now, I said, just so, curving
A little left, legs parted a little, and pulled a pillow
Under your belly, cool, just so, the slopes, the dip

And rise, parting your legs, I knelt a moment there
Viewing the line of you, so beautiful, your face
Hiding on your right arm. In a moment
You'll hear my heart on you and feel against the beat
Of your blood at the temple mine through your ruffled hair.

Heysham, rock tombs

These four sunk side by side in a rock table
Their shapes have filled with rain and in the wind
That blew their dust into the Pennine streams
They shiver so much we can't see how we'd look
Staring up at clouds, migrations, empty blue.

A love of churches

At sixteen I switched to Early Communion
Because it was shorter, but soon quitted for good
Because, like Saint Anthony
I could not keep my mind off the doings of the night before
But I never did lose my love of churches

Large and small but especially the small
Crouched low among their graves and however ancient
Predated by their yews, the font
Tapping deep into Terra, the nested corbels
Still exhibiting every degree of scurrility

And capitals, pews and choir stalls affirming the faith
In mermaids, centaurs, undines, green men
Whose eloquent gobs run over
Into boundless foliage. And now
Here's another house I could worship in Sunday mornings

And not renounce Saturday nights: that column
Garlanded in a rising or descending spiral
Pushing up through a helix of scallops
Is cold stone, but give me your hand
Let me fit the sunrise, the comb, the mound to your palm

Slope your long fingers down over the promontory
Feel the stone warm, my palmer
Many ancient ways are still new to us
There is much still to learn setting out from a place like this
Where the sea licks the windows.

Romanesque

The stairs are in the wall so you must climb
Like plant life shooting blindly for the light
And in an upper room, sun slanting through
There you will find me carved on a capital

A thousand years ago with glaring eyes
Parting two rods of growth that spring between
My planted feet and through this V sign mouthing
At her carved on the capital opposite

The mermaid who has split her tail and each
Fluke end of it is gently held aloft
By a centaur either side while she opens
Her braids, clearing her face for vision.

In the aerial room, in the round-arched window
Sun on your back, sit still and contemplate
The man-creature you love and who loves you
Enthralled in stone a thousand years ago.

A Romanesque church in the Rouergue

This god's house has roomy eaves up under which
Swallows and sparrows house alongside corbels
Which are themselves very lively. From ground level
Tilting the wishful head back I begin to feel
Up under there might be where I belong.

No one under that roofing expects to be still
Or sleep the sleep of the just, the good eight hours
And there must be others in bad nights with bitten fingers
Who find an end and undo the lovely intricate
Basketwork and drift off unravelling and who

Like me would be lost but for a sleeper-by
To tether and haul me home, plait me back in
Her pattern. Many dawns for half a century now
I have woken in places close under the eaves
Already flurrying with lascivious sparrows

So why shouldn't my gob spout tendrils? I want
The good opinion of the mermaid, I want
Her whispering across to the centaur, Perhaps
After all he remembers me and the sea
Perhaps I may still interest him in miscegenation

Sideways into plant-life and some of the other shapes
Of being creaturely. Up there no one forgets
How hungry the birdlife is, how every day
It must hunt and pilfer or die and that every brood
Of hatched desires insistently wants feeding.

Biped looking up, cityman lugging your longings
South or it might be west, north, east,
I will ride you like an incubus away from here
Away from the placid orchards, the kitchen gardens
And the acre in which the locals plant their dead.

Roman sarcophagus of a man and wife, Salerno Cathedral

Dressed marble slabs, four walls, a floor, a lid
Fitted together tight, harder than bone
Hard and implacable as the summons that
The messenger, light as a swallow, swooped

Under their lintel with. Brute marble fact
How they have softened it! How languidly
He poses leaning on his dipped-out torch
Two of him (there are two of them) and how

Within that frame, between those minders, stone,
A frieze, is moved to impersonate the sea
All running, curling, not one level line,
The dance and effervescence of the sea

Lifting for a festival: women astride
Horn-blowing tritons, naked, tugging the drenched
Beard round to have the mouth or sliding down
The chute of fish-coils, sea facilitating

The squirms of scale and skin, and flighted cupids
Showing them in mirrors. The buried pair
Unlidded long ago, blown down the winds,
Thanks be to them now for their furious horns

The squeals of Eros undulant through warm blood
The roar and bubbling of the sea. Observing
Love's fluid mutiny against the fact
Nonchalant Hermes surely envies them.

NOTES

'**Old Town**' (12) is a very free version – a transposition into my home town – of the Fado song 'Lisboa Antiga'.

'**Baucis and Philemon**' (41): this and the next four poems are free versions of stories in Ovid, trees being important in all of them.

'**A Faiyum death mask**' (97): Faiyum is a district of Middle Egypt where many Romano-Egyptian mummy portraits have been found.

'*Tomba 736...*' (88): Enotria (or Œnotria: 'wine-land'), is a district of Southern Italy, roughly modern Basilicata, much settled by the Ancient Greeks.

'**Red on black**' (89): Bologna stone is a phosphorescent form of barite (barium sulphate) first found near Bologna in the seventeenth century.